ETHEREUM – THE NEXT GENERATION OF CRYPTOCURRENCY

A GUIDE TO THE WORLD OF ETHEREUM

SATO AKIRA

Copyright © Sato Akira
All Rights Reserved.

ISBN 978-1-63920-508-0

This book has been published with all efforts taken to make the material error-free after the consent of the author. However, the author and the publisher do not assume and hereby disclaim any liability to any party for any loss, damage, or disruption caused by errors or omissions, whether such errors or omissions result from negligence, accident, or any other cause.

While every effort has been made to avoid any mistake or omission, this publication is being sold on the condition and understanding that neither the author nor the publishers or printers would be liable in any manner to any person by reason of any mistake or omission in this publication or for any action taken or omitted to be taken or advice rendered or accepted on the basis of this work. For any defect in printing or binding the publishers will be liable only to replace the defective copy by another copy of this work then available.

Contents

Preface   v

1. Main Purpose Of Ethereum   1
2. Difference Between Bitcoin And Ethereum   2
3. What Can Ethereum Be Used For   3
4. Ethereum - Guide For Beginners   8
5. How To Get Ether   13
6. Why Is Ethereum Needed   16
7. What Are The Risks Of Ethereum   19
8. The Ethereum Blockchain   21
9. How Ethereum Works   26
10. How To Make Money With Ethereum   28
11. Ethereum - Most Valuable   30
12. Benefits   34
13. Tips   37
14. How To Use   40
15. Other Crypto - Currencies   42
16. Wrap Up   45
17. Some Definitions   46
18. Conclusion   47

Disclaimer   49

Preface

In the times that we are living in, technology has made unbelievable advancement as compared to any time in the past. This evolution has redefined the life of man on almost every aspect. In fact, this evolution is an ongoing process and thus, human life on earth is improving constantly day in and day out. One of the latest inclusions in this aspect is ***Cryptocurrencies.***

Cryptocurrency is nothing but digital currency, which has been designed to impose security and anonymity in online monetary transactions. It uses cryptographic encryption to both generate currency and verify transactions. The new coins are created by a process called mining, whereas the transactions are recorded in a public ledger, which is called the **Transaction Block Chain.**

Evolution of cryptocurrency is mainly attributed to the virtual world of the web and involves the procedure of transforming legible information into a code, which is almost uncrackable. Thus, it becomes easier to track purchases and transfers involving the currency. Cryptography, since its introduction in the WWII to secure communication, has evolved in this digital age, blending with mathematical theories and computer science. Thus, it is now used to secure not only communication and information but also money transfers across the virtual web.

Ethereum is an open-source, public, blockchain-based distributed computing platform and operating system featuring smart contract (scripting) functionality. It supports a modified version of Nakamoto consensus through transaction based state transitions.

PREFACE

Ethereum has led the crypto world for so long, and so dominantly that the terms crypto and Ethereum are often used interchangeably. However, the truth is, the digital currency does not only comprise of Ethereum. There are numerous other crypto currencies that are part of the crypto world.

Ether is a cryptocurrency whose blockchain is generated by the Ethereum platform. Ether can be transferred between accounts and used to compensate participant mining nodes for computations performed. Ethereum provides a decentralized Turing-complete virtual machine, the Ethereum Virtual Machine (EVM), which can execute scripts using an international network of public nodes. "Gas", an internal transaction pricing mechanism, is used to mitigate spam and allocate resources on the network.

Ethereum was proposed in late 2013 by *Vitalik Buterin*, a cryptocurrency researcher and programmer. Development was funded by an online crowdsale that took place between July and August 2014. The system went live on 30 July 2015, with 11.9 million coins "premined" for the crowdsale. This accounts for approximately 13 percent of the total circulating supply.

Ethereum was initially described in a white paper by Vitalik Buterin, a programmer involved with Bitcoin Magazine, in late 2013 with a goal of building decentralized applications.Buterin had argued that Bitcoin needed a scripting language for application development. Failing to gain agreement, he proposed development of a new platform with a more general scripting language.

At the time of public announcement in January 2014, the core Ethereum team was Vitalik Buterin, Mihai Alisie, Anthony Di Iorio, and Charles Hoskinson. Formal development of the Ethereum software project began through a Swiss company, Ethereum Switzerland GmbH (EthSuisse). Subsequently, a Swiss non-profit foundation, the Ethereum Foundation (Stiftung Ethereum), was created as well. Development was funded by an online public crowdsale, with the participants buying the Ethereum value token (ether) with another digital currency, bitcoin. While there was early praise for the technical innovations of Ethereum, questions were also raised about its security and scalability.

One of Ethereum's most well known creators, Vitalik Buterin describes Ethereum as a "world computer". Ethereum can be accessed by anyone in the world with an internet connection, and users can interact with its computational features without permission. Ethereum can be used for data storage, financial transactions, land ownership and much more both imagined and yet to be imagined.

Ethereum isdecentralized;a record of all Ethereum transactions are stored on thousands of different computers around the world. In traditional systems, data is far more centralized, and it can become enormously expensive to achieve the same level of distribution (and thus security) that is enabled by Ethereum.

Ethereum istrusted;thanks to cryptographic signatures and complex mathematics, Ethereum can be interacted without a third party. Information entered into the network is immutable (will not change) and ownership of said information can be proven by its rightful owner.

Ethereum ispseudonymous;with cryptographic signatures, users who own information on Ethereum do not need to release personally identifiable information to prove their ownership. Transacting value across the Ethereum network can be done pseudonymously, and personal details can be revealed only if the sender chooses to do so.

Ethereum isfast;storing and transferring data on Ethereum can happen in seconds, whilst retaining the trust, privacy and decentralized (secure) fundamentals with which Ethereum provides. Once the protocol fully matures and the Ethereum application layer is established, the system will provide utility that is several orders of magnitudes greater than alternative options today.

Of course, Ethereum is still a very young technology. It was launched and is still working through a number of upgrades focused on scaling the protocol. However, in its short existence it has made progress at a phenomenal rate. The network value has risen from thousands of dollars to billions in its short lifetime, and this guide will help you to understand what Ethereum has the potential to achieve in the near future.

Ethereum is basically software that is decentralized and allows developers and programmers to run the code of any application. Ethereum has become a popular cryptocurrency alternative to Bitcoin over the last year. However, unlike Bitcoin and rival currency Litecoin, Ethereum has been adopted by many companies and startups as a way to transact (and more).

In the cryptocurrency wars, I like to view Ethereum like the diamond of the currencies - it has both a intrinsic value and an industrial value. Compare this to Bitcoin, which operates like gold - not much industrial value, but people buy it and sell it based on it is intrinsic value to the holder.

Given the popularity of Ethereum, many people are curious about what it actually is, how it is different than

Bitcoin, and how to invest in it. It is also important to note the risks of investing, and the potential to mine it and create your own wealth of Ether (the actual monetary unit of Ethereum).

Ethereum is an open-source, public, blockchain-based distributed computing platform featuring smart contract (scripting) functionality, which facilitates online contractual agreements. It provides a decentralized Turing-complete virtual machine, the Ethereum Virtual Machine (EVM), which can execute scripts using an international network of public nodes. Ethereum also provides a cryptocurrency token called "ether", which can be transferred between accounts and used to compensate participant nodes for computations performed. "Gas", an internal transaction pricing mechanism, is used to mitigate spam and allocate resources on the network. Ethereum was proposed in late 2013 by Vitalik Buterin, a cryptocurrency researcher and programmer.

The currency was launched in 2015, and although it is less than two years on the market, it has already become Bitcoin's top rival.

Bitcoin and Ethereum can provide significant advantages, especially in today's socioeconomic realities. However, keep in mind that this guide is not by any mean intended to be used as financial advice. I am not a financial advisor. I am just an active participant who has Bitcoin and cryptocurrencies in my investment portfolio with a bullish outlook on its future. And I want to share this with you because I believe it is the kind of information we can all benefit from one day. , one thing is very clear to me: Bitcoin, Ethereum, and cryptocurrencies are the new gold rush. So, do not get left behind! Now is your chance to become a millionaire.

ONE

Main Purpose of Ethereum

Unlike Bitcoin, the main purpose of Ethereum is not to act as a form of currency but to enable "smart contracts" between the parties without forcing them to trust or use a middleman. Smart contracts are computer codes that can facilitate the exchange of money, property, content, or anything of value. Because these contracts run on the blockchain, they run just as they are planned without any possibility of downtime, censorship or fraud.

Ethereum enables developers to build decentralized applications (or Dap.) Because these computer programs are made up of code that runs on a blockchain network, they aren't controlled by a central entity.

Think of Ethereum as the world's first decentralized virtual supercomputer.

TWO
DIFFERENCE BETWEEN BITCOIN AND ETHEREUM

Just like Bitcoin, Ethereum is an open-source blockchain network. Although there are some differences between them, the most relevant distinction you must remember is that they have different purposes.

Bitcoin offers just a particular application of the blockchain technology and is designed as a peer-to-peer system that facilitates digital transactions. Ethereum, on the other hand, is a platform for running applications on a distributed network that allows smart contracts between individuals worldwide.

THREE

WHAT CAN ETHEREUM BE USED FOR

First and foremost, Ethereum allows developers to build and deploy decentralized applications. Moreover, any centralized services can be decentralized using the Ethereum platform. The potential of Ethereum platform for building apps not limited by anything other than the creators' creativity.

Decentralized applications have a potential of changing the relationship between companies and their audiences completely. These days there are a lot of services that charge commission fees for simply providing an escrow service and a platform for users to trade goods and services. On the other hand, Ethereum's Blockchain's can enable customers to trace the origins of product they are buying, while the implementation of smart contracts can ensure safe and fast trading for both parties without any intermediary.

The Blockchain technology itself has a potential of revolutionizing web-based services as well as industries with long-established contractual practices. For example, an insurance industry in the US possesses more than $7 bln inclined life insurance money, which can be redistributed fairly and transparently using Blockchain. Moreover, with the implementation of smart contracts, clients can be able to simply submit their insurance claim online and receive an instant automatic payout, considering that their claim met all the re?uired criteria.

Essentially, the Ethereum Blockchain is capable of bringing its core principles - *trust, transparency, securityand efficiency* - into any service, business or an industry.

Ethereum can also be used to create Decentralized Autonomous Organizations (DAO), which operate completely transparently and independently of any intervention, with no single leader. DAOs are run by programming code and a collection of smart contracts written on the Blockchain. It is designed to eliminate the need for a person or a group of people in complete and centralized control of an organization.

DAOs are owned by people who purchased tokens. However, the amount of purchased tokens does not equate equity shares and ownership. Instead, tokens are contributions that provide people with voting rights.

Advantages of ethereum

Ethereum platform benefits from all the properties of the Blockchain technology that it runs on. It is completely immune to any third party interventions, which means that all the decentralized apps and DAOs deployed within the network can not be controlled by anyone at all.

Any Blockchain network is formed around a principle of consensus, meaning that all the nodes within the system need to agree on every change made within it. This eliminates possibilities of fraud, corruption and makes the network tamper-proof.

The whole platform is decentralized, which means there is no possible single point of failure. Hence, all the apps will always stay online and never switch off. Moreover, the decentralized nature and cryptographic security make the Ethereum network well protected against possible hacking attacks and fraudulent activities.

Disadvantages of Ethereum

Despite the fact that smart contracts are meant to make the network fault-proof, they can
only be as good as the people writing the code for them. There is always room for human error, and any mistake in the code might get exploited. If that happens, there is no direct way to stop a hacker attack or an exploitation of said mistake. The only possible way of doing so would be to reach a consensus and rewrite an underlying code. However, this goes completely against the very essence of the Blockchain, as it is supposed to be an unchangeable and immutable ledger.

What apps were developed on Ethereum?

Ethereum has a potential of opening up the world of decentralized apps even for people without any technical background. If this happens, it can become a revolutionary leap for Blockchain technology that will bring it closer to mass-adoption. Currently, the network can be easily accessed through its native Mist browser, which provides a user-friendly interface as well as a digital wallet for storing and trading Ether. Most importantly, users can write, manage and deploy smart contracts. Alternatively, Ethereum network can be accessed through a MetaMask extension for Google Chrome and Firefox.

The Ethereum platform has the potential of profoundly disrupting hundreds of industries that currently depend on centralized control, such as insurance, finance, real estate and so on. Currently, the platform is being used to create decentralized apps for a broad range of services and industries. Below is a list of some of the most noticeable ones.

Some of the ethereum platforms;

- **Gnosis**— A decentralized prediction market that enables users to vote on anything from the weather to election results.
- **EtherTweet**— This application takes its functionality from Twitter, providing users with a completely uncensored communication platform.
- **Etheria**— It feels and looks very much like Minecraft, but exists entirely on the Ethereum Blockchain.
- **Weifund** — An open platform for crowdfunding campaigns that implements smart contracts.
- **Uport**— Provides users with a self-sovereign ID that enables them to collect verifications, log-in without passwords, digitally sign transactions and interact with Ethereum apps.

- **Provenance**— The project aims to create an open and accessible framework of information for consumers to make informed decisions on their purchases. This is done through tracing the origins and histories of products.
- **Augur**— An open-source prediction and forecast market that rewards correct predictions.
- **Alice**— A platform that aims to bring transparency to social funding and charity through Blockchain technology.
- **Bitnation**— The World's First Virtual Nation, a Blockchain jurisdiction. It contains many of the same functions as a traditional nation, such as insurance, education, ID cards, diplomacy programmes, including ones for ambassadors and for refugees and many many more.
- **Ethlance**— A freelance platform to exchange work for Ether rather than any other currencies.

FOUR
Ethereum - Guide for Beginners

In order to fully understand Ethereum, what it does and how it can potentially impact our society, it is important to learn what its core properties are and how they differ from standard approaches.

First of all, Ethereum is a decentralized system, which means it is not controlled by any single governing entity. An absolute majority of online services, businesses and enterprises are built on a centralized system of governance. This approach has been used for hundreds of years, and while history proved time and time again that it is flawed, its implementation is still necessary when the parties do not trust each other.

A centralized approach means single-entity control, but it also means a single point of failure, which makes apps and online-servers utilizing this system extremely vulnerable to hacker attacks and even power outages. Moreover, most social networks and other online servers require users to provide at least some degree of personal information, which is then stored on their servers. From there, it can be easily stolen by the company itself, its rogue workers or hackers.

Ethereum, being a decentralized system, is fully autonomous and is not controlled by anyone at all. It has no central point of failure, as it is being run from thousands of volunteers' computers around the globe, which means it can never go offline. Moreover, users' personal information stays on their own computers, while content, such as apps, videos, etc., stays in full control of its creators without having to obey by the rules imposed by hosting services such as App Store and YouTube.

Secondly, it is important to understand that even though constantly compared to each other, Ethereum and Bitcoin are two completely different projects with entirely different goals. Bitcoin is the first ever cryptocurrency and a money-transfer system, built on and supported by a distributed public ledger technology called the Blockchain.

Ethereum took the technology behind Bitcoin and substantially expanded its capabilities. It is a whole network, with its own Internet browser, coding language and payment system. Most importantly, it enables users to create decentralized applications on Ethereum's Blockchain.

Those applications can either be entirely new ideas or decentralized reworks of already existing concepts. This essentially cuts out the middleman and all the expenses associated with the involvement of a third party. For example, the only profit that comes from users 'liking' and 'sharing' their favorite musician's posts on Facebook is generated from an advertisement placed on their page and it goes directly to Facebook. In an Ethereum version of such social network, both the artists and the audience would receive awards for positive communication and support. Similarly, In a decentralized version of Kickstarter, you will not be getting just some artifact for your contribution to the company, you will be receiving a part of the company's future profits. Finally, Ethereum-based applications will remove all sorts of payments to third parties for fascinating any kind of services.

In short, Ethereum is a public, open-source, Blockchain-based distributed software platform that allows developers to build and deploy decentralized applications.

As it was mentioned before, Ethereum is a decentralized system, which means it utilizes a peer-to-peer approach. Every single interaction happens between and is supported only by the users taking part in it, with no controlling authority being involved.

The entire Ethereum system is supported by a global system of so-called '*nodes.*' Nodes are volunteers who download the entire Ethereum's Blockchain to their desktops and fully enforce all the consensus rules of the system, keeping the network honest and receiving rewards in return.

Those consensus rules, as well as numerous other aspects of the network, are dictated by 'smart contracts.' Those are designed to automatically perform transactions and other specific actions within the network with parties that you do not necessarily trust. The terms for both parties to fulfill are pre-programmed into the contract. The completion of these terms then triggers a transaction or any other specific action. Many people believe that smart contracts are the future and will eventually replace all other contractual agreements, as the implementation of smart contracts provides security that is superior to traditional contract law, reduce transaction costs associated with contracting and establish trust between two parties.

Moreover, the system also provides its users with the Ethereum Virtual Machine (EVM), which essentially serves as a runtime environment for smart contracts based on Ethereum. It provides users with security to execute an untrusted code while ensuring that the programs do not interfere with each other. EVM is completely isolated from the main Ethereum network, which makes it a perfect sandbox-tool for testing and improving smart contracts.

The platform also provides a cryptocurrency token called 'Ether.'

Whocreated Ethereum?

In late 2013, Vitalik Buterin described his idea in a white paper, which he sent out to a few of his friends, who in turn sent it out further. As a result, about 30 people reached out to Vitalik to discuss the concept. He was waiting for critical reviews and people pointing out critical mistakes in the concept, but it never happened.

The project was publicly announced in January 2014, with the core team consisting of Vitalik Buterin, Mihai Alisie, Anthony Di Iorio, Charles Hoskinson, Joe Lubin and Gavin Wood. Buterin also presented Ethereum on stage at a Bitcoin conference in Miami, and just a few months later the team decided to hold a crowdsale of Ether, the native token of the network, to fund the development.

IsEthereum a cryptocurrency?

By definition, Ethereum is a software platform that aims to act as a decentralized Internet as well as a decentralized app store. A system like this needs a currency to pay for the computational resources required to run an application or a program. This is where *'Ether'* comes into play.

Ether is a digital bearer asset and it does not require a third party to process the payment. However, it does not only operate as a digital currency, it also acts as 'fuel' for the decentralized apps within the network. If a user wants to change something in one of the apps within Ethereum, they need to pay a transaction fee so that the network can process the change.

The transaction fees are automatically calculated based on how much 'gas' an action requires. The amount of required fuel is calculated based on how much computing power is necessary and how long it will take to run.

IsEthereum like Bitcoin?

Ethereum and Bitcoin might be somehow similar when it comes to the cryptocurrency aspect, but the reality is that they are two completely different projects with completely different goals. While Bitcoin has established itself as a relatively stable and the most successful cryptocurrency to date, Ethereum is a multipurpose platform with its digital currency Ether being just a component of its smart contract applications.

FIVE
How to Get Ether

There are two primary ways of obtaining Ether: buying it and mining it.

The most common and perhaps the most convenient way of buying Ether is buying it on exchanges. All you need to do is find an exchange that trades in Ether and operates within your jurisdiction, set up an account and use either your bank account, wire transfer or in some cases even your bank card to buy Ether tokens. Those will then need to be stored in a wallet, which can be provided by an exchange itself, Ethereum's native Mist browser or by various other specialized services.

Alternatively, you can obtain Ether through peer-to-peer trading, paying for it with any agreed upon currency, including Bitcoin and other cryptocurrencies. This can be done both online and in-person. Peer-to-peer trading is rather popular among Bitcoin users. However, due to the virtually unlimited supply of Ether tokens and the Ethereum platform not putting complete user anonymity at the forefront of the system, Ether is usually obtained via exchanges.

Another way of getting Ether tokens is by mining them. Mining Ethereum uses proof-of-work, which means that miners contribute their computing power to solve a complex mathematical problem in order to 'seal-off' and confirm a block of actions within the network. Miners who manage to successfully complete this task receive a reward for every block mined.

What makes Ether valuable?

In simple terms, the price of Ethereum is driven by demand. Investors buy Ethereum in the hope that the technology expands and improves leading to further increased demand (driven by utility) and a return on investment. Those who want to interact with the Ethereum blockchain or to move money out of the fiat system (for reasons not limited to the above) will also push the price higher. Ethereum is valuable because it provides a better solution to the status quo, currently its two most valuable use cases are fundraising and financial transactions. However there is another type of technology enabled by Ethereum which could upend the existing global tangle of digital infrastructure.

Smart Contracts

Ethereum is described as a "world computer" because transactions can initiate sets of functions which carry out automated and guaranteed tasks. For example, a transaction from Alice to Contract Y could run through a function inside the contract which then sends the transaction from Contract Y to Bob. A simple example of a function inside this smart contract would be an escrow, where the funds are released to Bob once certain conditions are met, and Bob can be certain he will be paid. Smart contracts can be linked together to contract a web of automated value transfers which trigger based on prior agreed terms. This technology has the potential to disrupt global finance on an unprecedented level, but even more importantly, smart contracts will also enable machine to machine payments in the AI driven economy of the future. Ethereum is currently the most utilized and valuable smart contract platform in the industry, however other platforms do also exist. Bitcoin has a smart contract layer called "Rootstock" and NEO is a blockchain similar to Ethereum which is gaining traction in China. Other smart contract platforms to be aware of include Cardano and EOS.

SIX
WHY IS ETHEREUM NEEDED

Through the lens of the status quo, it is very easy to consider the technology of today to be "good enough". Often it is difficult to imagine how protocols can upend global socioeconomics; in the same way that when the TCP/IP protocol of the Internet was built, few – if any – could have predicted where things would be just a few decades later. Ethereum is somewhat similar, however with the Internet already established globally, this new technology is capable of spreading and being adopted much faster than anything ever seen before. Ethereum will fundamentally change certain aspects of our lives, and in the years to come, we will – as we are now with the Internet – surprised that we ever lived without it.

Peer to peer

The role of the trusted middleman is a relatively new concept. Careers have been built around functions that require third parties to help settle transactions between multiple groups or individuals. The need for a middleman has been essential, and the role has been responsible for unprecedented economic growth in the 20th century. It has also been responsible for economic catastrophe. Ethereum removes the middleman from a vast array of transactions and contracts. Rather than trusting a 3rd party who may (knowingly or unknowingly) fail in their duty as a middleman, people can trust computer code. So long as an individual has faith in the laws of mathematics, they can have faith in Ethereum's ability to execute whatever transaction was agreed to by two parties. This removal of the middleman achieves enormous advantages in the form of security, speed and efficiency (low cost). In the current state of Ethereum, such transactions are mostly limited to the world of financial payments, however as the technology grows, this application is expanding to much more complex agreements between parties.

Sovereignty

Most people in developed nations take wealth sovereignty for granted. Legal tender issued by governments and central banks ensures that your hard earned dollars can be spent on goods and services. There are two key hazards to this which Ethereum solves:

Opaque MonetarySupply

How many dollars exist in circulation today? No one has an exact answer to that question. The printing press is hard at work on the judgement of a few to devalue existing holdings and to incentivize spending, without providing transparent figures by how much and to what extent. At the time of writing, it is certain that the number of Ethereum tokens in existence today is 96,331,928, and there will be roughly 3 new tokens every 15 seconds moving forward. This is all trackable on Ethereum's transparent blockchain – which is described in more detail further below.

Ownership Rights

The history of humanity has a poor record of protecting individual ownership. Financial transactions have always been and still are at the mercy of a few, and the wealth of an individual can be arbitrarily dissolved overnight. This problem is far more of an issue in developing nations, particularly those which have experienced civil war and corruption. The most recent crisis in Syria highlights this; where middle class and low income families looking to flee the country lose their wealth as they cross the border. Ethereum solves this problem in two ways; first of all, property rights and other forms of ownership can (in the near future) be publicly verifiable on the Ethereum blockchain. In more practical and immediate terms however, wealth stored on the Ethereum blockchain cannot be confiscated. Freedom from confiscation is an essential tenet of cryptocurrencies like Ethereum, and through its use, families can take sovereignty over their own wealth and gain global mobility without the trade-off in standard of living.

SEVEN

WHAT ARE THE RISKS OF ETHEREUM

The risks of Ethereum are known and unknown (in the case of a "black swan event") and there are risks to both users and investors. This guide will touch upon the most critical risks to the ecosystem, and further details will be discussed in this article on "what could destroy the price of Ethereum?".

Platform Risk

Ethereum has faced DDoS attacks in the past however the network has sustained an impressive 100% uptime. The Ethereum blockchain itself is highly secure and funds stored on the blockchain face very low platform risk.

Application Risk

The largest attack vector on the Ethereum blockchain has been at the application layer and not the protocol layer as described above. Smart contracts have been exploited on several occasions, with multi-million-dollar exploits being relatively common (these links are certainly not exhaustive).

Users and investors should be very cautious when dealing with Ethereum applications – the code is guaranteed to execute in its specified manner, however the specification may well have been flawed.

RegulatoryRisk

Ethereum has built a positive reputation among the mainstream media, however the continued success of its platform will eventually come as a threat to many governments and central banks. The risk of heavy handed regulation looms over the cryptocurrency space and Ethereum is no exception. Regulatory risk could see both user and investor funds being difficult to exchange for fiat currency, however the likelihood of this happening so far at least seems small. In addition to that, Ethereum has a strong leadership group (Ethereum Foundation) which has made significant inroads with promoting the technology as a cause for good.

EIGHT

THE ETHEREUM BLOCKCHAIN

Blockchain became a buzzword in 2017, several years after it was first described in Satoshi Nakamoto's famous Bitcoin whitepaper. On the Bitcoin blockchain, transactions in the network are bundled together and stored in blocks, with each block referencing the previous one, all the way back to the first generated block, known as the "genesis block".

This chain of connected blocks became known as the blockchain; essentially a ledger of all transactions which have ever taken place. The blockchain is stored across thousands of computers (called "Nodes") which agree on the history of the Bitcoin network and its consensus rules. By distributing the blockchain in this way, the risk of shutting down the system is mitigated.

The Ethereum blockchain is built in much the same way. Every transaction, whether to another individual's wallet or smart contract, is recorded on its public blockchain. Each transaction broadcast to the network is also processed (validated) by every node on the network to ensure that it follows consensus rules. This means that a single transaction to perform any arbitrary function would need to be executed once for every node on the network. This type of validation brings enormous security to the network, however it has a considerable trade-off with scalability. Software upgrades to improve the scalability of the network whilst retaining this key feature of security are well underway for Ethereum.

Blockchain Stakeholders

There are a number of stakeholders within the blockchain ecosystem. These are:

- *Nodes*
- *Light Clients*
- *Exchanges*
- *Miners*

Nodes

The role of the node is to enforce consensus rules and validate transactions. This covers multiple facets; as one example, a node would validate the balance of an account ensuring that a transaction plus its "gas" fee (transaction fee) is not to be greater than the balance. A transaction which did not validate would simply be ignored and not included in a block therefore failing to be recorded in the agreed ledger.

Light Clients

Most Ethereum wallets are "light clients". Unlike a node, a light client does not store a full or pruned copy of the Ethereum blockchain. Instead, these light clients connect to nodes to receive relevant data about the state of the blockchain, allowing the user to safely transact on the network without the complexities of running a node. The size of the Ethereum blockchain is many gigabytes large; light clients allow users to use the Ethereum blockchain without having to download, store and process a copy of every transaction ever created.

Exchanges

Exchanges are the on and off ramps to and from Ethereum and fiat currency (USD, EUR, GBP etc). Exchanges operate outside of the blockchain, however some decentralized crypto-to-crypto exchanges are being built which operate using smart contracts on the Ethereum blockchain. An exchange is a third party private enterprise, and storing funds in an exchange has its own risks.

Miners

Miners secure the network by bundling valid transactions together into blocks, connecting each new block with the one previously forming immutable history of Ethereum transactions and balances (known as the "state"). This is the blockchain. Finding a block rewards the successful miner with three Ether plus the transaction fees of every transaction inside that block.

To mine a block, the miner must provide a "Proof of Work" to satisfy a condition. The condition is that the hash of the block is below a certain target. The target is set in such a way that to meet the condition, the miner must have spent work solving it "Proof of Work". The target is dynamic, making the condition easier or more difficult to reach depending on how much effort is being put in by the miners. Through mathematics, the target ensures that on average a new block will be found every 12 seconds. If less effort is being spent mining, the target will adjust to become easier, ensuring that the average block time remains at 12 seconds.

A simple analogy to Ethereum mining can be found in the rolling of dice. Assume the target set is to roll a six, 3 times in a row. Once you are successful, you provide proof that you rolled a six 3 times in a row and the network rewards you with Ether. In the case of Ethereum mining, the difficulty is closer to rolling a six dozens of times in a row, however the miners use powerful graphics cards to compute the "rolls" at many trillions of times per second.

Decentralized Applications

Smart Contracts have paved the way for "decentralized applications" or "dApps". Unlike traditional applications such as Uber or Facebook, a dApp is not owned by a company, instead its code is deployed to the Ethereum blockchain for anyone to run. By creating a dApp, the user does not need to trust a company to execute the terms of service; instead this is done by the smart contracts with which the dApp is built. Currently there are a few dApps on the market which are operational in some way today:

CryptoKitties

This dApp allows users to "breed" cats on the blockchain. Each cat is referenced by its own unique Ethereum address which makes up its genetic code. Cats are transferable and immutable. CryptoKitties was the first dApp to reach mainstream media in November 2017 and has provided inspiration for a host of new applications.

Etherisc

An insurance dApp which pays out its customers instantly through the Ethereum blockchain. This dApp uses oracles to determine outcomes of events, and pays out their customers accordingly. No trust from either party is required.

Augur

A prediction market dApp which allows users to create and bet on markets that reflect outcomes. Similar to Etherisc, Augur pays out each prediction market's winner instantly based on the outcome given by one or more oracles (third party sensors/APIs which digitize outcomes).

Code deployed to the Ethereum blockchain is open source and visible for anyone to copy and use as an example, you can see the code use for one of the CryptoKitties smart contracts here. The competitive advantage that dApp creators have is in the "front end" website that they build for users to interact with. CryptoKitties.co is the first great example of a simple front end experience which interacts with far more complex smart contracts under the hood. The complexities and usefulness of dApps will only expand, and it seems likely that the first mainstream Ethereum dApp will deploy within the next 5 years.

NINE
How Ethereum Works

As it was mentioned before, Ethereum is based on Bitcoin's protocol and its Blockchain design but is tweaked so that applications beyond money systems can be supported. The two Blockchains' only similarity is that they store entire transaction histories of their respective networks, but Ethereum's Blockchain does a lot more than that. Besides the history of transactions, every node on Ethereum network also needs to download the most recent state, or the current information, of each smart contract within the network, every user's balance and all the smart contract code and where it is stored.

Essentially, the Ethereum Blockchain can be described as a transaction-based state machine. When it comes to computer science, a state machine is defined as something capable of reading a series of inputs and transitioning to a new state based on those inputs. When transactions are executed, the machine transitions into another state.

Every state of Ethereum consists of millions of transactions. Those transactions are grouped to form 'blocks,' with each and every block being chained together with its previous blocks. But before the transaction can be added to the ledger, it needs to be validated, that goes through a process called mining.

Mining is a process when a group of nodes apply their computing power to completing a 'proof of work' challenge, which is essentially a mathematical puzzle. The more powerful their computer is, the quicker it can solve the puzzle. An answer to this puzzle is in itself a proof of work, and it guarantees the validity of a block.

A lot of miners around the world are competing with each other in an attempt to create and validate a block, as every time a miner proves a block new Ether tokens are generated and awarded to said miner. Miners are a backbone of the Ethereum network, as they not only confirm and validate transactions and any other operations within the network but also generate new tokens of the network's currency.

TEN
HOW TO MAKE MONEY WITH ETHEREUM

The technology that underlies Ethereum means that it can be used for a number of other purposes that will be built off of a decentralized and autonomous system. Simply put, it potentially will be a revolutionary technology with the potential to impact a whole spectrum of industries.

As the demand for the Ethereum platform and its smart contracts enabled network increases, the value of Ethereum as a cryptocurrency will continue to surge.

Stability – Ethereum had an organic growth, without massive spikes, and it seems to be stable, if not even predictable. The increasing demand and value of a certain cryptocurrency serve as an indicator of its potential. Whatever the reason is, it still increases the demand – meaning a further increase in Ethereum price.

The developers at Ethereum want one to think of the network as a large virtual computer that facilitates applications to run. It is indeed this allure that has been the reason that the project has got the backing from a number of individuals such as Bill Gates.

Making waves in the established industry: Microsoft offers Ethereum as a blockchain-as-a-service.

The second biggest market cap after Bitcoin only, and one of the most popular cryptocurrencies ever in terms of volume.

ELEVEN
ETHEREUM - MOST VALUABLE

Bitcoin is also credited with bringing blockchain technology into the mainstream. Blockchain is the digital and distributed ledger that underpins virtual currencies and is responsible for logging all transactions without the need for a financial intermediary, like a bank. It is expected to be a game changer for the financial services industry due to its ability to speed up transaction verification and settlement times, as well as lower transactions fees.

Blockchain is also anticipated to have utility well beyond the financial sector, with various technology and consumer goods companies using it to manage connected devices through the Internet of things or to more efficiently control a merchandise supply chain.

However, this investor does not believe bitcoin deserves its title as the world's most valuable cryptocurrency by market cap. Yes, its first to market advantage has some perks, as does its brand name among crypto enthusiasts. But bitcoin's focus on partnering with merchants to accept its token, rather than focusing on making its blockchain more enterprise friendly, could be its downfall. A shift in focus among cryptocurrencies has made it pretty clear that wrangling merchants takes a backseat in terms of long-term value creation relative to blockchain development and deployment. That is why Ethereum, the second largest cryptocurrency by market cap, deserves to be the most valuable digital currency.

Ethereum's focus is entirely on blockchain development and catering to businesses that could benefit from deploying blockchain. This means it is targeting banks that would relish cross-border transactions that complete in seconds or minutes compared to wait times of up to three to five days with the current banking system. A recent analysis from HowMuch.net found that Ethereum's network processes about 20 transactions per second compared to bitcoin at a maximum of seven transactions per second.

It also means that Ethereum's blockchain is being tested by technology, energy, and retail companies that could benefit from the efficiencies created by blockchain. Though bitcoin probably has a lot of merchants accepting its token as a form of payment, the Enterprise Ethereum Alliance, formed of recent, has about 200 member organizations currently testing a version of its blockchain technology.

First, the integration of smart contract protocols do make a difference. Smart contract protocols help to verify, facilitate, or enforce the negotiation of a contract, and they are particularly attractive to enterprises. The belief is that paper contracts are not very efficient, and they can sometimes be confusing or not legally binding. Smart contracts allow businesses to modify Ethereum's blockchain to make it as simple or complex as they choose, and they are legally binding. These smart contracts can function as multisignature accounts that determine when money can be spent, or they can simply be used to store information about an application.

The other factor that makes Ethereum light-years more attractive than bitcoin is that the Ethereum Virtual Machine (EVM) tends to be the basis of evolution for a number of burgeoning cryptocurrencies. Think of EVM as the environment that smart protocols operate in. For instance, Qtum combines the core infrastructure of bitcoin with EVM to allow enterprise customers the ability to fully dictate the complexity and scope of their smart contracts.

Perhaps the biggest issue relates to the emergence of blockchain technology. The buzz around blockchain is thick enough to cut with a knife, yet it is a technology that is technically been around for about a decade and is only now being demoed and tested in small-scale projects. Businesses are naturally moving slow with blockchain because it remains relatively unproven. In some cases, implementing blockchain would mean completely starting from scratch, suggesting it is a cumbersome and costly venture. In other words, there is no guarantee that these tests will result in a quick adoption of blockchain technology. History suggests that if blockchain is successful, it will take years to implement, which could quell the euphoria that is currently rampant among cryptocurrencies.

The barrier to entry is also exceptionally low when it comes to blockchain development. Even though that Ethereum is still the preferred blockchain choice of enterprises, a number of big companies have ventured out to create their own proprietary blockchain technology. For example, Cisco Systems (NASDAQ: CSCO) has created a blockchain capable of monitoring connected devices and determining the trustworthiness of new devices that connect to the network. Cisco has effectively paved a way to manage the Internet of Things.

TWELVE

BENEFITS

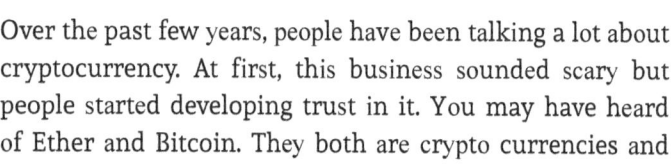

Over the past few years, people have been talking a lot about cryptocurrency. At first, this business sounded scary but people started developing trust in it. You may have heard of Ether and Bitcoin. They both are crypto currencies and use the Blockchain Technology for highest security possible. Nowadays, these currencies are available in several types.

As far as fraud is concerned, this type of currency can not be faked as it is in digital form and can not be reversed or counterfeited unlike the credit cards.

Immediate settlement

Buying real property involves third parties, such as lawyers and notary. So, delays can occur and extra costs may incur. On the other hand, Ethereum contracts are designed and enforced in order to include or exclude third parties. The transactions are quick and settlements can be made instantly.

Lower fees

Typically, there is no transaction fee if you want to exchange Ethereum or any other currency. For verifying a transaction, there are minors who get paid by the network.

Although there is zero transaction fee, most buyers or sellers hire the services of a third-party, such as Coinbase for the creation and maintenance of their wallets. If you do not know, these services function just like Paypal that offers a web-based exchange system.

Identification of theft

Your merchant gets your full credit line when you provide them with your credit card. This is true even if the transaction amount is very small. Actually, what happens is that credit cards work based on a "pull" system where the online store pulls the required amount from the account associated with the card. On the other hand, the digital currencies feature a "push" mechanism where the account holder sends only the amount required without any additional information. So, there is no chance of theft.

Open access

According to statistics, there are around 2.2 billion people who use the Internet but not all of them have access to the conventional exchange. So, they can use the new form of payment method.

Decentralization

As far as decentralization is concerned, an international computer network called Blockchain technology manages the database of Ethereum and Bitcoin. In other words, Ethereum is under the administration of the network, and there is no central authority. In other words, the network works on a peer-to-peer based approach.

Recognition

Since cryptocurrency is not based on the exchange rates, transaction charges or interest rates, you can use it internationally without suffering from any problems. So, you can save a lot of time and money. In other words, Ethereum and other currencies like this are recognized all over the world. You can count on them.

So, if you have been looking for a way to invest your extra money, you can consider investing in Ethereum. You can either become a miner or investor. However, make sure you know what you are doing. Safety is not an issue but other things are important to be kept in mind.

THIRTEEN
TIPS

Cryptocurrency is the newest trend in the money market that contains the elements of computer science and mathematical theory. Its primary function is to secure communication as it converts legible information into an unbreakable code. You can track your purchases and transfers with cryptocurrency. Following are the top ten tips for investors to invest in cryptocurrency. It is Just Like Investing in Commodities:

Investing in cryptocurrency is just like investing in any other commodity. It has two faces - it can be used as an asset or as an investment, which you can sell and exchange.

BuyEthereum Directly:

Buy Ethereum directly if you do not want to pay the fee for investing or if you are interested in possessing real Ethereum. There are a lot of options all over the world including Bitcoin.de, BitFinex, and BitFlyer from where you can buy Ethereum directly.

Onlyan Absolute MinorityUsesCryptocurrency:

Today, Ethereum is the most common cryptocurrency in the world of investment. In the some part of the world, only

24% of the adults know about it, and surprisingly only 2% Americans use it. It is good news for the financial investors as the low usage represents a fruitful investment for the future.

sage isGrowing:

The combined market cap of the cryptocurrencies is more than 60 billion American dollars. It includes all cryptocurrencies in existence including hundreds of smaller and unknown ones. The real-time usage of the cryptocurrencies has gone up, showing a rise in trend.

Usage is theKeyCriteria:

As an investor, the usage must be the key for you. The demand and supply data of cryptocurrencies exhibits a decent investment opportunity right now. There exists a strong usage of the currencies for facilitating payments between financial institutions and thus, pushing transaction costs down meaningfully.

The Market Cycle:

Currently, the cryptocurrency market is in euphoria. It is the point where the investment may not appear as a golden opportunity to you but the values will go higher from here. Businesses, governments, and society across the globe will soon be considering cryptocurrencies.

It will SolveProblemsfor You:

Money is to solve problems, and so is the cryptocurrency. The bigger problem it solves, the higher potential value it gets. The sweet spot for possessing cryptocurrency is that it provides access to money and basic bank functions including paying and wiring.

Crypto toMoney:

Today, cryptocurrencies can be exchanged to conventional paper money. Therefore, the lock-in risk that existed a while ago is gone now.

Create Your Portfolio:

Since cryptocurrencies are exchangeable, they have become another way to build your portfolio. You can now store cash in the form of crypto and exchange it for cash anytime you need the traditional money.

Read the Right Resources:

'Everyone and his uncle' becomes a guru during any hype. Be very skeptical while selecting reading sources and people who do cryptocurrency investment.

FOURTEEN
HOW TO USE

It is very easy for the ordinary people to make use of this digital currency. Just follow the steps given below:

You need a digital wallet (obviously, tostorethe currency)

Makeuseof the wallet to createuniquepublicaddresses(thisenables you toreceivethecurrency)

Use thepublic addresses totransfer funds in or out of thewallet

Cryptocurrency wallets

A cryptocurrency wallet is nothing else than a software program, which is capable to store both private and public keys. In addition to that, it can also interact with different blockchains, so that the users can send and receive digital currency and also keep a track on their balance.

Thewaythedigital walletswork

In contrast to the conventional wallets that we carry in our pockets, digital wallets do not store currency. In fact, the concept of blockchain has been so smartly blended with cryptocurrency that the currencies never get stored at a particular location. Nor do they exist anywhere in hard cash or physical form. Only the records of your transactions are stored in the blockchain and nothing else.

A real-life example

Suppose, a friend sends you some digital currency, say in form of ethereum. What this friend does is he transfers the ownership of the coins to the address of your wallet. Now, when you want to use that money, you have unlocked the fund.

In order to unlock the fund, you need to match the private key in your wallet with the public address that the coins are assigned to. Only when both these private and public addresses match, your account will be credited and the balance in your wallet will swell. Simultaneously, the balance of the sender of the digital currency will decrease. In transactions related to digital currency, the actual exchange of physical coins never take place at any instance.

Understanding the cryptocurrency address

By nature, it is a public address with a unique string of characters. This enables a user or owner of a digital wallet to receive cryptocurrency from others. Each public address, that is generated, has a matching private address. This automatic match proves or establishes the ownership of a public address. As a more practical analogy, you may consider a public cryptocurrency address as your eMail address to which others can send emails. The emails are the currency that people send you.

Understanding the latest version of technology, in form of cryptocurrency is not tough. One needs a little interest and spend time on the net to get the basics clear.

FIFTEEN
Other Crypto-Currencies

Bitcoin

Bitcoin is a type of electronic currency (CryptoCurrency) that is autonomous from traditional banking and came into circulation in 2009. According to some of the top online traders, Bitcoin is considered as the best known digital currency that relies on computer networks to solve complex mathematical problems, in order to verify and record the details of each transaction made. The Bitcoin exchange rate does not depend on the central bank and there is no single authority that governs the supply of CryptoCurrency. However, the Bitcoin price depends on the level of confidence its users have, as the more major companies accept Bitcoin as a method of payment, the more successful Bitcoin will become. Bitcoin is the first global, decentralized currency that allows you to send money from one person to another without involving a third party broker, such as a bank. You only need your computer to make transactions because Bitcoin is fundamentally software. As a decentralized currency, Bitcoin is not controlled by anyone. It is open so that anyone can benefit from it.

Zcash:

Zcash came out in the later part of 2016. The currency defines itself as: "if Ethereum is like http for money, Zcash is https".

Zcash promises to provide transparency, security, and privacy of transactions. The currency also offers the option of 'shielded' transaction so the users can transfer data in the form of encrypted code.

Dash:

Dash is originally a secretive version of Ethereum and Bitcoin. It is also known as 'Darkcoin' due to its secretive nature.

Dash is popular for offering an expanded anonymity which allows its users to make transactions impossible to trace.

The currency first appeared on the canvas of digital market in the year 2014. Since then, it has experienced a large fan following over a very short span of time.

Ripple:

With a market capitalization of over $1bn, Ripple is the least among list. The currency was launched in 2012 and offers instant, secure, and low-cost payments.

The consensus ledger of Ripple does not require mining, a feature which makes it different from Ethereum and other mainstream crypto currencies.

The lack of mining reduces the computing power which ultimately minimizes the latency and makes transactions faster.

SIXTEEN

WRAP UP

Although Bitcoin continues to lead the pack of crypto, the rivals are picking up the pace. Currencies like Ethereum and Ripple have surpassed Bitcoin in enterprise solutions and are growing in popularity each day. Going by the trend, the other cryptos are here to stay and will soon be giving Bitcoin a real tough time to maintain its stature.

SEVENTEEN

Some Definitions

- **Cryptocurrency**: electronic currency; also called digital currency.
- **Fiat money**: any legal tender; government backed, used in banking system.
- **Ethereum:** Is an open source, public, blockchain-based distributed computing platform and operating system featuring smart contract(Scripting) functionality.
- **Bitcoin**: the original and gold standard of crypto currency.
- **Altcoin:** other cryptocurrencies that are patterned from the same processes as Bitcoin, but with slight variations in their coding.
- **Miners**: an individual or group of individuals who use their own resources (computers, electricity, space) to mine digital coins.
- **Wallet:** a small file on your computer where you store your digital money.

EIGHTEEN

CONCLUSION

With many people losing hope in the traditional banking system, virtual currencies are beginning to become a more appealing and a better option for both consumers and companies. So, it should come as no surprise that Ethereum is increasing in value and is even considered aa reliable alternative to the gold standard.

Ethereum focuses on something new: it is not only about payments in electronic cash, it is also about the creation of smart contracts. So, while Bitcoin is a digital currency, Ethereum is a platform for running applications on a distributed network.

Disclaimer

Introduction

By using this book, you accept this disclaimer in full.

No advice

The book contains information. The information is not advice, and should not be treated as such.

No representations or warranties

To the maximum extent permitted by applicable law and subject to section below, we exclude all representations, warranties, undertakings and guarantees relating to the book.

Without prejudice to the generality of the foregoing paragraph, we do not represent, warrant, undertake or guarantee:

- that the information in the book is correct, accurate, complete or non-misleading;

- that the use of the guidance in the book will lead to any particular outcome or result.

Limitations and exclusions of liability

The limitations and exclusions of liability set out in this section and elsewhere in this disclaimer: are subject to section 6 below; and govern all liabilities arising under the disclaimer or in relation to the book, including liabilities arising in contract, in tort (including negligence) and for breach of statutory duty.

We will not be liable to you in respect of any losses arising out of any event or events beyond our reasonable control.

We will not be liable to you in respect of any business losses, including without limitation loss of or damage to profits, income, revenue, use, production, anticipated savings, business, contracts, commercial opportunities or goodwill.

We will not be liable to you in respect of any loss or corruption of any data, database or software.

We will not be liable to you in respect of any special, indirect or consequential loss or damage.

Exceptions

Nothing in this disclaimer shall: limit or exclude our liability for death or personal injury resulting from negligence; limit or exclude our liability for fraud or fraudulent misrepresentation; limit any of our liabilities in any way that is not permitted under applicable law; or exclude any of our liabilities that may not be excluded under applicable law.

Severability

If a section of this disclaimer is determined by any court or other competent authority to be unlawful and/or unenforceable, the other sections of this disclaimer continue in effect.

If any unlawful and/or unenforceable section would be lawful or enforceable if part of it were deleted, that part will be deemed to be deleted, and the rest of the section will continue in effect.

Law and jurisdiction

This disclaimer will be governed by and construed in accordance with Swiss law, and any disputes relating to this disclaimer will be subject to the exclusive jurisdiction of the courts of Switzerland.

www.ingramcontent.com/pod-product-compliance
Lightning Source LLC
Chambersburg PA
CBHW020709180526
45163CB00008B/3012